ISBN 978-1-332-91971-0
PIBN 10472620

1 MONTH OF
FREE
READING

at

www.ForgottenBooks.com

By purchasing this book you are eligible for one month membership to ForgottenBooks.com, giving you unlimited access to our entire collection of over 1,000,000 titles via our web site and mobile apps.

To claim your free month visit: www.forgottenbooks.com/free472620

English
Français
Deutsche
Italiano
Español
Português

www.forgottenbooks.com

Mythology Photography **Fiction**
Fishing Christianity **Art** Cooking
Essays Buddhism Freemasonry
Medicine **Biology** Music **Ancient**
Egypt Evolution Carpentry Physics
Dance Geology **Mathematics** Fitness
Shakespeare **Folklore** Yoga Marketing
Confidence Immortality Biographies
Poetry **Psychology** Witchcraft
Electronics Chemistry History **Law**
Accounting **Philosophy** Anthropology
Alchemy Drama Quantum Mechanics
Atheism Sexual Health **Ancient History**
Entrepreneurship Languages Sport
Paleontology Needlework Islam
Metaphysics Investment Archaeology
Parenting Statistics Criminology
Motivational

ernet Archive
ston Scanning Center

pment ID

ꓱ #

Bulletin 364   July, 1946

THE UNIVERSITY OF NEW HAMPSHIRE

AGRICULTURAL EXPERIMENT STATION

Department of Agricultural and Biological Chemistry

Inspection of Commercial Feedingstuffs

Made for the

State Department of Agriculture

By T. O. Smith and H. A. Davis

The University of New Hampshire

Durham, N. H.

INSPECTION OF COMMERCIAL FEEDINGSTUFFS
MADE FOR THE
STATE DEPARTMENT OF AGRICULTURE

The inspection of commercial feedingstuffs reported in this bulletin was made under the direction of Honorable Andrew L. Felker, Commissioner of Agriculture. Mr. C. A. Lyon, Feed Control Supervisor, with the assistance of Mr. David Allen and Mr. George Laramie, Inspectors, collected samples of 348 brands of feedingstuffs which were offered for sale in the state during the year ending June, 1946. The 348 samples represent brands of 79 manufacturers.

REGISTRATION AND LABELING OF FEEDINGSTUFFS

Registration:- - The New Hampshire law, entitled an Act to Regulate the Sale of Commercial Feedingstuffs, requires registration with the Commissioner of Agriculture of each brand offered for sale. This is usually done by the manufacturer or jobber whether he is located within or outside the State. Feedingstuffs manufactured in other states frequently pass through several middlemen before they reach the local distributor. Under the provisions of the law, if the manufacturer or jobber fails to make registration, the dealer is responsible. Dealers who purchase feed for resale must assure themselves that the brands they purchase are properly registered and the license fee is paid or they must assume that responsibility. The official charged with the administration of the law is the Commissioner of Agriculture. All matters relative to registration and all inquiries concerning the law should be addressed to the Commissioner of Agriculture, State House, Concord.

Labeling:—The law requires every manufacturer or dealer who shall sell or offer for sale any concentrated commercial feedingstuff to furnish with each package a clearly printed statement certifying the net weight of the feed contained in the package, the brand name or trademark under which the feed is sold, the name and address of the manufacturer, the ingredients of which the feed is composed, and a chemical analysis stating the minimum percentage only of protein and of fat and the maximum percentage only of crude fiber. In order to secure greater uniformity in the labeling of feeds and in the statement of ingredients, the Association of American Feed Control Officials has adopted definitions and standards. The Association has also approved 23 general regulations which "should be adopted by state officials as far as the statutes will permit." There are no conflicts with the New Hampshire feedingstuffs law in these regulations. Manufacturers and dealers are, therefore, expected to conform to the regulations of the Association in all matters not specifically mentioned in the law.

One sentence in the New Hampshire feedingstuffs law reads as follows: " . . . and shall state in bold type upon the container or tag attached thereto, if a compounded feed, the names of the several ingredients therein contained." To avoid the misinterpretaton or

3

deception which may result from the manufacturer's use of indefinite terms in listing the ingredients, the Association of American Feed Control Officials has adopted 196 official definitions of ingredients used in the compounding of feedingstuffs. These definitions are subject to frequent addition and revision. At the present time there are also 27 tentative definitions and six that have been proposed for future discussion. Tentative definitions are those which have received favorable consideration but have not yet been made official. A 99-page booklet containing the above three classes of definitions, 23 general regulations, four tentative regulations, 25 resolutions adopted and other instructive material may be obtained from the Secretary of the Association of American Feed Control Officials, College Park, Maryland. The manufacturer should secure a copy of this booklet and list the ingredients accurately. Carelessness or indifference in listing the ingredients should create sales resistance in the buyer. The purchaser is warranted in concluding that the manufacturer who is inaccurate in specifying the ingredients printed on the tag may be careless in selecting the ingredients he puts into the bag.

PURPOSE OF THE FEEDINGSTUFFS LAW

The chief purpose of the feedingstuffs law is to protect the consumer against the inferior products which doubtless would soon appear on the market if the trade were not under state control. The law is primarily a correct-labeling act. It must not be assumed by the purchaser of feedingstuffs that every brand which meets the manufacturer's guarantee is a high-grade feed. The feedingstuffs law does not prevent the sale of a low-grade feed if it is properly licensed and tagged and is offered for sale in compliance with the law. It would not be in the public interest to legislate against the sale of the lower-grade by-products. They can be fed profitably if bought at a price adjusted to their feeding value. The law does prevent an inferior feed being offered for sale as a high-grade product.

The dealer, in purchasing feed from the manufacturer, and the consumer, in purchasing feed from the dealer, should make the specification that the feed delivered must comply with the New Hampshire feedingstuffs law. If the feed is not registered; if the protein, fat, and crude fiber are not guaranteed; and if the ingredients of which the feed is composed are not plainly stated on the bag, or on a tag attached thereto, the purchaser is not protected by the state feedingstuffs law. He then has no recourse under the feedingstuffs law if the feed which he purchases is of inferior quality. The dealer who offers for sale a feedingstuff which has not been registered and which is not guaranteed in compliance with the law is probably indifferent to his customer's interests in other respects. He does not merit either the confidence or the patronage of the consumer. The purchaser's cooperation in refusing to buy a feed which does not conform to the law in every respect will not only help in the enforcement of the law but will at the same time afford the purchaser himself the protection of the law. If the buyer fails to assure himself that the legal requirements have been met, he accepts the feedingstuff at his

4

own risk. The terms used in reporting the chemical analysis of a feedingstuff are briefly defined as follows:

Protein is a collective term for a considerable group of compounds, all of which contain nitrogen. Ingredients high in protein are usually more expensive than the other ingredients, making protein the most important nutrient for consideration in determining the commercial value of a feedingstuff. The nutritional value of the proteins varies widely; therefore, a feedingstuff should contain protein from several sources to insure inclusion of all essential types.

Fat is separated from the other components of a feedingstuff by extracting the moisture-free sample with anhydrous ether. In such ingredients as the cereals, the seed-meals, and animal products, the extract is nearly pure fat. A few ingredients such as alfalfa meal contain some ether-soluble material which is not fat. When urea is present the figure for the percentage of fat found may be high as much as two-tenths per cent, due to the slight solubility of urea in anhydrous ether. When sulphur is present the percentage of fat found is much too high, since sulphur is readily soluble in anhydrous ether.

Fiber is composed of cellulose and related compounds. Since crude fiber has little feeding value, the law requires that the maximum fiber be guaranteed rather than the minimum as in protein and fat.

This bulletin is concerned with the enforcement of the feedingstuff law. It is not within its scope to make recommendations regarding the use of commercial feedingstuffs. The Department of Dairy Husbandry and the Department of Poultry Husbandry are continuously studying feeding problems. The following publications of these departments are free to residents of New Hampshire. Address your request to Mail Service, University of New Hampshire, Durham, New Hampshire.

Ext. Cir. 195	Adjusting Feed Costs to Reduced Milk Incomes. 4 pp.
Ext. Cir. 208	Feeding Dairy Calves and Heifers. 6 pp.
Folder 10	The Use of Home-grown Grains in Feeding the Dairy Herd.
Press Bull. 100	Home-Grown Dairy Feeds. 1 p.
Ext. Bull. 67	Turkey Production in New Hampshire. 16 pp.
Ext. Cir. 158	Feeding Chickens. 18 pp.
Ext. Cir 250	The Home Poultry Flock. 12 pp.
Sta. Bull. 312	Protein Requirements of Chickens. 20 pp.
Sta. Bull. 335	Protein Requirements of Chickens at Various Stages of Growth and Development II. 15 pp.
Sta. Cir. 52	Growth and Feed Standards for New Hampshire. 8 pp.
Sta. Cir. 56	Fine Verus Coarse Grit as a Feed Ingredient for Poultry. 8 pp.

While the word feedingstuff does not appear in all the above titles, no publication is included which does not discuss some aspect of the use of feedingstuffs.

HOW COST OF INSPECTION AFFECTS PRICE

The cost of a feedingstuff inspection includes the drawing and the analysis of the samples, and the publication and mailing of the annual bulletin. The funds from which these costs are paid are accumulated from the license fees which the manufacturer is required to pay annually on each brand of feedingstuff offered for sale within the state. Since manufacturing and distributing costs are finally paid by the consumer, the purchaser of feedingstuffs is interested in the effect of the cost of the inspection on the retail price per ton. The sixteenth census of the United States Department of Commerce under the heading, specified farm expenditures, 1939, reports the retail value of feeds for domestic animals and poultry sold in New Hampshire in that year as $7,619,245. A calculation based on this valuation and on the known costs of the inspection shows that the cost to purchasers is less than four cents per ton of feed, a fraction of a cent per 100-pound bag. The 1939 figure for the retail value of feedingstuff sold annually in the state is used, since it is the most recent authoritative figure available. It is estimated the present figure is more than double that amount. If the estimated valuation is used, the cost of the inspection is less than two cents per ton.

CONFORMITY TO THE GUARANTEES

Of the 348 brands analyzed, 91 brands, or 26.1 per cent, were below the guaranteed amount of protein. Thirty of these were less than one-half per cent below guarantee. Thirty-nine brands, or 11.2 per cent, were below guarantee in fat. Eight of these were less than one-fourth per cent below guarantee. Fifty-one brands, or 14.6 per cent, contained an excessive amount of crude fiber.

Resolution 20, p. 14 of the Official Publication of the Association of American Feed Control Officials, referred to above reads in part "that urea is to be used only in such limited quantities as to insure that the total amount present does not exceed 3% of the (grain) ration." Five brands contained urea as one of the ingredients. None exceeded the 3 per cent urea permitted under the resolution.

In the tabulaton of the analytical figures (p. 10 to p. 19 inclusive) those figures one-half per cent or more below guarantee in protein, one-fourth per cent or more below guarantee in fat, and one per cent or more above guarantee in crude fiber are printed in bold face type.

Table I shows the percentage of samples failing to conform to the guarantee in each of the last 21 years.

TABLE I		**PERCENTAGE OF SAMPLES ANALYZED**		

<table>
<tr><td colspan="6" align="center">TABLE I   PERCENTAGE OF SAMPLES ANALYZED
IN YEARS 1926-1946 NOT CONFORMING TO GUARANTEES</td></tr>
<tr>
<th rowspan="3">Year</th>
<th colspan="2">Per cent below
guarantee in Protein</th>
<th colspan="2">Per cent below
guarantee in Fat</th>
<th rowspan="3">Per cent high
in Crude Fiber</th>
</tr>
<tr>
<th>Less than
0.5 per cent</th>
<th>0.5 per cent
or more</th>
<th>Less than
0.25 per cent</th>
<th>0.25 per cent
or more</th>
</tr>
<tr><td></td><td></td><td></td><td></td></tr>
<tr><td>1926</td><td>8.0</td><td>16.0</td><td>4.0</td><td>10.0</td><td>6.0</td></tr>
<tr><td>1927</td><td>8.3</td><td>16.4</td><td>5.8</td><td>13.6</td><td>5.9</td></tr>
<tr><td>1928</td><td>9.1</td><td>20.7</td><td>4.3</td><td>9.3</td><td>7.9</td></tr>
<tr><td>1929</td><td>9.5</td><td>20.2</td><td>2.8</td><td>9.3</td><td>6.5</td></tr>
<tr><td>1930</td><td>4.8</td><td>13.1</td><td>4.0</td><td>8.0</td><td>3.9</td></tr>
<tr><td>1931</td><td>1.8</td><td>7.2</td><td>5.9</td><td>9.7</td><td>5.3</td></tr>
<tr><td>1932</td><td>1.8</td><td>1.4</td><td>5.0</td><td>8.1</td><td>2.8</td></tr>
<tr><td>1933</td><td>1.3</td><td>3.6</td><td>7.5</td><td>9.8</td><td>3.6</td></tr>
<tr><td>1934</td><td>3.0</td><td>3.4</td><td>3.9</td><td>7.1</td><td>9.8</td></tr>
<tr><td>1935</td><td>2.4</td><td>3.0</td><td>4.2</td><td>8.5</td><td>9.9</td></tr>
<tr><td>1936</td><td>2.9</td><td>5.2</td><td>5.5</td><td>8.3</td><td>12.2</td></tr>
<tr><td>1937</td><td>2.8</td><td>4.2</td><td>3.0</td><td>6.0</td><td>11.0</td></tr>
<tr><td>1938</td><td>2.9</td><td>8.1</td><td>9.8</td><td>10.8</td><td>11.5</td></tr>
<tr><td>1939</td><td>1.9</td><td>3.3</td><td>6.8</td><td>9.3</td><td>8.7</td></tr>
<tr><td>1940</td><td>2.9</td><td>4.0</td><td>6.2</td><td>6.7</td><td>7.5</td></tr>
<tr><td>1941</td><td>1.1</td><td>2.6</td><td>4.7</td><td>6.7</td><td>5.6</td></tr>
<tr><td>1942</td><td>2.6</td><td>3.5</td><td>3.7</td><td>4.5</td><td>7.4</td></tr>
<tr><td>1943</td><td>3.7</td><td>2.7</td><td>7.7</td><td>8.6</td><td>7.4</td></tr>
<tr><td>1944</td><td>8.2</td><td>9.0</td><td>10.7</td><td>19.7</td><td>6.9</td></tr>
<tr><td>1945</td><td>2.1</td><td>6.1</td><td>2.9</td><td>7.5</td><td>7.1</td></tr>
<tr><td>1946</td><td>8.6</td><td>17.5</td><td>2.3</td><td>8.9</td><td>14.6</td></tr>
</table>

REQUEST BY INDIVIDUALS FOR THE ANALYSIS
OF FEEDINGSTUFFS

Under the feedingstuffs law the Agriculture Experiment Station is charged only with the analysis of samples of feedingstuffs collected by the State Inspector under the direction of the Commissioner of Agriculture. It does, each year, however, analyze a considerable number of samples drawn by individuals representing stock purchased by them for their own use. Frequently the reason for sending the sample is that the feed is suspected of causing sickness or death of livestock or poultry. While in very rare instances the feed may have caused the trouble, disease is usually found to be the cause. Many times feeders, suspecting the feed, lose valuable time in the treatment of the disease by sending a sample of the feed for analysis and waiting for the report. Losses could have been reduced had a veterinarian or poultry specialist been consulted immediately and proper treatment given promptly. The most conclusive method of determining whether or not the feed is the cause of the trouble is a biological test. Such a test can be conducted on the premises of the feeder. If chicks have died and the feed is suspected, confine in sanitary pens two lots of healthy chicks. Give to one lot the suspected feed and to the other lot a feed known to be good. Should the chicks receiving the suspected feed become ill and the others remain healthy, there is evidence the feed is the cause. Under such circumstances, notify the Commissioner of Agriculture and an official sample will be drawn. The official sample will be analyzed to determine if the manufacturer is responsible.

The most common reason the purchaser has for asking to have the sample analyzed is to satisfy himself whether the feed meets its guarantee and if it does not, to obtain evidence upon which to base a claim for shortage. The Station can assume no responsibility for the drawing of an unofficial sample but can attest only the accuracy of the analysis of the sample as submitted. It is practically impossible to secure a representative sample of a feedingstuff composed of several ingredients varying widely in composition without the aid of a sampling tube for drawing the sample and proper equipment for mixing it. A feed may contain as one of its ingredients gluten meal averaging 40 per cent protein, and as another ingredient oat mill feed averaging 5 per cent protein. These materials are so different in physical condition that the shaking in transit tends to seperate them even though they may have been perfectly mixed by the manufacturer before bagging. It is apparent that an accurate sample of a ton of this feed can only be had by drawing a core from several bags. The official method requires ten. Since a representative sample is as essential as an accurate analysis in judging the value of a shipment of feed, it is evident that a satisfactory adjustment can seldom be effected on the basis of an unofficial sample.

Notwithstanding the objections which may be raised to the analysis of samples taken without proper sampling equipment, the Station is disposed to continue this work as long as there is evidence that it constitutes a useful service. The samples so submitted should be drawn from at least ten bags in a manner which will insure that the small lot sent for analysis is as accurately representative as possible of the large lot from which it is taken. Because of the cost of laboratory work and materials, an analysis is not usually warranted on a sample drawn from less than a one-ton lot of feed.

A one-pound sample is sufficient for the analysis. It should be sent in a glass jar or tin box to prevent loss of fine particles and a change in the moisture content. In order that the department may have a record of the sample analyzed, and may know whether or not the manufacturer and the dealer are complying with the requirements of the law, the following information should be submitted concerning each sample.

Brand ....

Manufacturer ....

Address ....

Guarantee:

        Protein ....

        Fat ....

        Crude Fiber ....

Ingredients ....

....

....

Dealer ....

Address ....

Number of bags in lot ....

Number of bags sampled ....

Price per 100 pounds ....

Your name ....

Your address ....

Your reason for requesting analysis ....

....

Manufacturer	Pounds in 100 lbs. of Feedingstuff					
Brand	Protein		Fat		Crude Fiber	
	Guaranteed*	Found	Guaranteed*	Found	Guaranteed*	Found
Acme Milling Co.						
Olean, New York						
Acme Golden Broiler Mash	20.00	**14.10**	3.00	4.05	8.00	6.73
Acme Golden Dairy Feed	18.00	**12.28**	3.50	3.83	9.00	7.59
Acme Golden Mash for Laying Hens	20.00	**14.76**	3.00	4.59	7.00	7.91
Acme Golden Starter Mash	20.00	**13.64**	3.00	3.76	7.00	6.13
Allied Mills						
Chicago, Illinois						
Wayne All Mash Breeder	15.00	17.42	3.0	3.17	7.00	5.51
Wayne All Mash Egg	15.00	17.60	2.5	3.35	8.00	7.60
Wayne Chick Starter	20.00	21.54	3.0	4.26	7.00	6.97
Wayne 20% Dairy Ration	20.00	21.36	3.0	3.79	10.00	8.62
Wayne Egg Mash	20.00	20.79	3.00	4.18	8.00	6.89
Wayne Fitting Ration	12.00	14.49	3.0	4.31	9.00	8.20
Wayne Growing Mash	16.00	17.21	3.0	5.22	8.00	7.54
Wayne Pork Maker	14.00	16.07	3.0	3.32	7.00	5.43
Wayne Ranch Meal	17.00	18.78	3.50	4.76	7.50	5.88
Allison & Company						
Elkhart, Illinois						
Tabor's Broiler Ration	18.00	**15.79**	3.00	3.74	7.00	4.85
American Maize Products Co.						
Roby, Indiana						
Amaizo Gluten Meal	41.00	44.56	1.00	2.97	6.00	5.17
Anadarko Alfalfa Mill						
Anadarko, Oklahoma						
Alfalfa Meal	13.50	15.19	1.50	1.54	32.00	29.94
Archer-Daniels-Midland Co.						
Minneapolis, Minnesota						
ADM Flax Plant By-Product	5.00	6.44	1.50	1.98	50.00	44.48
Archer Old Process 34% Protein Lin-						
seed Oil Meal	34.00	34.72	3.50	5.88	9.00	8.01
Ashcraft Wilkinson Co.						
Atlanta, Georgia						
Cow-Eta Brand 41% Protein Cotton-						
seed Oil Meal	41.00	41.20	5.00	6.51	13.00	9.94
E. W. Bailey & Co.						
Montpelier, Vermont						
Bailey's Pennant Breeder Mash	20.00	20.23	3.00	4.90	7.00	6.38
Bailey's Pennant Calf Ration	15.00	16.11	3.00	4.22	8.50	8.47
Bailey's Pennant Chick Starter	18.00	18.17	3.00	3.73	6.50	5.78
Bailey's Pennant Complete Egg Ration	16.00	14.92	3.00	3.42	7.00	7.56
Bailey's Pennant Complete Grower	15.00	15.41	3.00	3.46	7.00	7.68
Bailey's Pennant 16% Dairy Ration	16.00	18.17	3.00	4.23	8.00	8.00
Bailey's Pennant Fitting Ration	14.00	16.16	3.00	4.67	7.50	7.66
Bailey's Pennant Growing Mash	18.00	18.39	3.00	4.23	7.00	6.84
Bailey's Pennant Horse Feed	10.50	11.03	3.00	3.58	9.00	6.13
Bailey's Pennant Laying Mash	20.00	19.68	3.00	3.77	7.00	7.62
Bailey's Pennant Turkey Fattener ..	18.00	15.09	3.00	3.99	6.00	4.55
Bailey's 14% Utility Feed	14.00	14.19	3.00	4.02	7.50	**10.16**
Pig Feed	17.00	**16.26**	3.00	3.36	7.00	5.57
Beacon Milling Co.						
Cayuga, New York						
"16" Auburn	16.00	15.28	3.25	3.29	10.00	8.72
Beacon Breeders' Mash	22.00	23.03	3.50	5.44	7.50	7.42
Beacon C-C Pellets	15.00	17.29	1.00	7.84	5.00	4.62

*Protein and fat not less than, crude fiber not more than.

Manufacturer Brand	Pounds in 100 lbs. of Feedingstuff					
	Protein		Fat		Crude Fiber	
	Guaranteed*	Found	Guaranteed*	Found	Guaranteed*	Found
Beacon Milling Co. Concluded						
Beacon Broiler Feed	20.00	21.71	3.00	4.78	7.00	6.92
Beacon Calf Grain	14.00	15.28	4.00	4.59	10.00	8.56
Beacon Calf Starter	19.00	18.30	3.50	4.43	7.00	5.75
Beacon Cayuga Horse Feed	10.00	13.31	2.50	3.68	9.00	7.52
Beacon Chick Feed	10.00	11.82	3.00	3.71	2.50	1.70
Beacon Complete Starting Ration ..	20.00	22.90	3.00	5.59	6.50	7.40
Beacon Duck Fattener	14.00	16.64	3.50	3.93	5.50	5.49
Beacon Fitting Ration	14.00	14.80	3.50	3.94	8.00	8.76
Beacon Fleshing Pellets	20.00	20.75	3.00	5.55	7.50	6.83
Beacon Growing Mash	18.00	18.73	3.00	4.58	7.50	7.54
Beacon Special 18	18.00	21.32	3.50	4.26	9.00	8.43
Beacon Test Cow Ration	18.00	18.82	4.00	4.12	9.00	8.06
Beacon Turkey Growing Mash	20.00	21.98	3.00	4.71	7.00	7.08
L. Clayton Berry Lebanon, New Hampshire						
Colonial Dairy Ration	14.00	16.68	3.50	4.27	12.00	7.98
Blue Banner Feed Co. East St. Louis, Illinois						
Blue Banner Laying Mash	18.00	17.64	3.50	4.00	7.50	8.04
Cokato Mill and Elevator Co. Cokato, Minnesota						
Gibraltar 16% Dairy Ration	16.00	17.90	4.00	3.92	8.00	7.98
Gibraltar 18% Egg Mash	18.00	19.48	4.50	3.77	6.00	7.51
Colebrook Feed Co. Colebrook, New Hampshire						
Colebrook 16% Dairy Ration	16.00	18.25	3.50	3.52	8.00	8.97
Commander-Larrabee Milling Co. Minneapolis, Minnesota						
Sunfed Wheat Bran	14.00	16.51	4.00	4.93	12.00	9.43
O. A. Cooper Co. Humboldt, Nebraska						
Copper's Best Grain Mix	9.50	9.85	3.00	3.65	3.00	2.02
Poultry Base Mix	9.50	8.49	3.00	3.86	3.00	3.40
Succulent Dairy Feed	11.00	10.50	1.60	1.55	24.00	19.22
Cooper's 18% Egg Mash	18.00	16.85	3.00	3.69	8.00	6.81
Cooperative Alfalfa Mills Big Bend, Colorado						
Alfalfa Meal	15.00	16.42	1.50	1.73	32.00	29.99
Corn Products Refining Co. New York, New York						
Buffalo Corn Gluten Feed	23.00	24.91	2.00	3.10	8.50	8.09
Charles M. Cox Co. Boston, Massachusetts						
Wirthmore Breeder Mash	20.00	19.91	3.00	3.34	7.00	5.25
Wirthmore Calf Starter Meal	22.00	22.50	3.50	3.71	6.00	5.41
Wirthmore Complete Breeder Ration	15.00	15.67	3.00	3.83	6.00	4.57
Wirthmore Complete Egg Ration ...	15.00	16.64	3.00	3.42	6.00	4.47
Wirthmore Complete Growing Ration	15.00	16.77	3.00	3.72	7.00	4.53
Wirthmore Complete Growing Ration (Pelleted)	15.00	15.85	3.00	3.28	7.00	5.01
Wirthmore Fitting Ration	14.00	15.06	4.00	4.33	8.00	6.24
Wirthmore Growing Mash	17.50	18.04	3.00	4.01	7.00	5.77
Wirthmore Horse Feed	10.00	12.04	3.25	4.32	9.00	9.79
Wirthmore Laying Mash	20.00	21.10	3.00	3.64	7.00	5.27

*Protein and fat not less than, crude fiber not more than.

| Manufacturer | Pounds in 100 lbs. of Feedingstuff | | | | | |
| Brand | Protein | | Fat | | Crude Fibe | |
	Guaranteed*	Found	Guaranteed*	Found	Guaranteed*	Foun
Charles M. Cox Co. Concluded						
Wirthmore Rabbit Pellets	14.00	15.89	3.0	4.69	15.00	10.7
Wirthmore 16 Record Ration	16.00	17.86	3.50	4.13	8.00	6.6
Wirthmore Standard 16 Dairy	16.00	16.24	3.0	3.24	10.00	5.8
Wirthmore Standard 20 Dairy	20.00	22.16	3.0	3.53	8.50	9.3
Wirthmore Starter and Broiler Ration	20.00	17.32	3.00	3.76	6.50	5.7
Wirthmore Stock Feed	10.00	10.24	3.0	3.52	11.00	10.3
Wirthmore Turkey Fattening Ration	16.00	17.90	3.0	3.53	7.00	4.2
Wirthmore Turkey Growing Ration..	20.00	20.31	3.00	3.74	7.00	4.7
Crawford Brothers Walton, New York						
Crawford Producer	18.00	20.27	3.50	3.96	10.00	5
Crawford Turkey Marketing Feed ..	12.00	14.71	4.00	4.20	7.00	5.2
Crete Mills Crete, Nebraska						
Triumph Egg Mash	17.50	17.10	3.50	4.36	7.50	8.2
Victor Broiler Mash	19.00	18.56	4.00	4.73	8.50	7.9
Victor Chick Mash	18.50	17.63	4.50	5.06	7.50	7.6
Dailey Mills Olean, New York						
Milk Producer 18%	18.00	18.19	4.00	4.13	10.00	8.
Delaware Mills Deposit, New York						
Delaware Breeder Mash	20.00	16.80	3.00	4.10	8.00	5.
Delaware Egg Mash	18.00	20.92	3.00	4.32	9.00	7.
Delaware Fitting Ration	14.00	15.94	4.00	4.54	10.00	7.
Delaware Growing Mash	18.00	20.58	3.00	4.81	7.00	6.
Delaware Horse Feed	9.00	11.38	3.00	4.14	10.00	9.
Delaware Laying Mash	20.00	20.18	3.00	4.66	8.00	7.
Delaware Scratch Grains	10.00	10.28	2.00	2.52	4.00	3.
Delaware Starter and Broiler Ration	18.00	20.49	3.50	4.74	7.00	6.
Delaware Starter Grower Layer	17.00	17.86	3.00	5.15	7.00	5.
Delaware Sweet 20% Dairy Feed	20.00	20.53	4.00	4.75	10.00	9.
Indian Sweet 20% Dairy Feed	20.00	21.41	3.00	4.19	11.00	9.
Dietrich & Gambrill Frederick, Maryland						
Pen Mar 16% Dairy	16.00	17.73	3.50	5.21	10.00	10.
Dodge Grain Co. Methuen, Massachusetts						
Dodge Starting Growing Mash	16.00	16.07	4.00	4.04	10.00	7.
Eagle Roller Mill Co. New Ulm, Minnesota						
Eagle Wheat Bran with Screenings ..	14.00	15.72	4.00	5.25	12.00	10.
Eagle Wheat Mixed Feed with Screenings	15.00	16.72	4.00	5.33	9.50	7.
Eastern States Farmers' Exchange West Springfield, Massachusetts						
Eastern States All Mash Developer	14.50	14.71	2.50	3.54	6.50	5.
Eastern States All Mash Egg	14.50	16.90	2.50	3.70	6.50	6.
Eastern States Breeder Concentrate Pellets	20.00	20.39	3.5	4.95	8.00	6.
Eastern States Calf Starter	23.00	23.25	3.00	3.37	6.00	5.
Eastern States Calving Ration	10.00	10.68	1.5	2.24	18.00	13.
Eastern States Developer	18.00	17.69	2.5	3.76	8.00	7.
Eastern States Egg Mash	20.00	19.74	2.5	3.91	8.00	6.

*Protein and fat not less than, crude fiber not more than.

12

Pounds in 100 lbs. of Feedingstuff

and

	Protein		Fat		Crude Fiber	
	Manufacturer					

Eastern States Ex. Concluded

	Protein		Fat		Crude Fiber	
stern States Fitting Ration	14.00	16.59	3.	3.91	10.00	8.36
stern States Fulpail	18.00	18.34	3.	4.47	9.00	6.68
stenr States Pork Builder	15.00	14.86	2.	3.56	6.50	4.49
stern States Sheep and Goat	16.00	17.38	3.	3.87	8.00	6.39
stern States Sixteen	16.00	16.55	3.	4.67	9.00	7.51
stenr States Starting and Broiler	18.00	18.08	2.00	3.73	7.00	5.21
stern States Turkey Grower Pellets	18.00	18.39	2.00	3.66	7.50	5.85

Elmore Milling Co.
Oneonta, New York

	Protein		Fat		Crude Fiber	
more Before and After Calving tion	12.00	13.97	3.50	3.69	10.00	13.61
more Complete Layer and Breeder	15.00	15.94	3.50	3.22	8.00	6.27
more Complete Market Egg Mash	15.00	15.98	3.50	4.36	8.00	7.43
more Complete Starter Broiler	20.00	20.48	3.50	4.63	7.00	7.48
more Fitting Ration	14.00	16.81	4.00	4.21	10.00	11.52
more Fleshing Pellets	15.00	16.64	3.50	4.54	8.00	9.69
more Growing Mash	18.00	17.51	3.50	4.39	8.00	9.80
more M. A. C. Laying Mash	18.00	17.31	3.50	4.81	8.00	8.31
more Milk Grains Sixteen	16.00	21.89	4.00	4.71	10.00	9.55
more Milk Grains Twenty	20.00	19.27	4.00	4.38	10.00	8.41
more Stock Feed	9.00	8.67	3.00	3.25	13.00	17.18
ranger 20% Dairy Ration	20.00	22.07	3.50	4.47	11.00	12.29

John W. Eshelman & Sons
Lancaster, Pennsylvania

	Protein		Fat		Crude Fiber	
ennsy 16 Dairy Feed	16.00	18.47	3.00	4.25	11.00	8.69
ed Rose 16 Dairy	16.00	18.61	4.00	5.33	11.00	8.85
ed Rose Growing	16.00	17.77	3.50	4.18	7.50	7.19
ed Rose Laying Mash	20.00	20.92	3.50	3.66	7.50	7.42

Farmers Feed Co.
New York, New York

	Protein		Fat		Crude Fiber	
ull Brand Dried Brewers' Grains ..	26.00	30.60	5.00	6.76	17.00	12.28

Federal Mill
Lockport, New York

	Protein		Fat		Crude Fiber	
airy Maid Wheat Mixed Feed	13.50	14.58	3.50	4.51	8.50	8.14

E. H. Felton & Co.
Indianola, Iowa

	Protein		Fat		Crude Fiber	
lue Belt Egg Mash	18.00	18.43	3.50	3.75	7.00	6.35

Finger Lakes & Hudson Flour Mills
Geneva, New York

	Protein		Fat		Crude Fiber	
angaroo Standard Wheat Bran	15.00	14.28	4.00	4.08	12.00	9.47

Flory Milling Co.
Bangor, Pennsylvania

	Protein		Fat		Crude Fiber	
loco Sugared Stock Feed	10.00	9.87	2.50	1.27	11.00	8.03
lory Breeder Mash	21.00	22.33	4.00	4.08	7.50	7.31
lory Broiler Mash	20.00	20.58	4.00	4.27	7.00	5.74
lory 16% Dairy Feed	16.00	18.12	3.00	3.73	10.00	8.58
lory Fattener and Flesher Pellets	14.00	14.40	5.00	3.79	7.00	6.09
lory Ftting Ration	14.00	16.59	2.50	2.55	10.00	8.63
lory Free Range Growing Mash ..	16.00	16.20	3.00	4.12	7.50	6.23
lory 18% Growing Mash	18.00	19.74	4.00	3.74	7.50	5.63
lory Hog Feed	16.00	11.99	3.50	3.30	9.00	8.98
lory Laying Mash	19.00	17.21	4.00	3.19	7.50	7.22
lory Rabbit Pellets	14.00	16.81	3.00	3.63	9.00	6.26
lory 18% Test Ration	18.00	21.45	4.00	3.74	10.00	7.92

*Protein and fat not less than, crude fiber not more than.

Manufacturer / Brand	Pounds in 100 lbs. of Feedingstuff					
	Protein		Fat		Crude Fiber	
	Guaranteed*	Found	Guaranteed*	Found	Guaranteed*	Found
General Mills **Detroit, Michigan**						
Dried Beet Pulp	7.00	8.62	0.30	0.36	22.50	20.64
Farm Service Breeder Mash	19.00	19.87	3.00	4.63	9.50	7.67
Farm Service Growing Mash	18.00	20.31	3.50	4.37	8.00	7.12
Farm Service Horse Feed	9.00	10.81	3.00	4.51	9.50	8.93
Farm Service Laying Mash Pellets	20.00	19.35	3.50	3.75	8.50	5.91
Farm Service Starter and Broiler	18.00	20.23	3.50	4.25	8.50	8.44
Farm Service Stock Feed	8.50	9.89	3.50	3.70	12.50	13.78
Larro Breeder Mash Pelleted	20.00	20.44	3.00	4.29	8.00	6.35
Larro Calf Builder	24.00	25.74	3.50	5.19	8.00	3.97
Larro Chick Builder	19.00	20.84	3.00	3.65	7.00	5.91
Larro 18% Dairy Feed	18.00	19.70	3.00	3.84	12.00	10.00
Larro 18% Egg Mash	18.00	18.95	3.00	4.15	8.00	6.47
Larro 19% Turkey Finisher	19.00	20.40	3.00	3.89	7.50	5.97
Oat Mill Feed	3.50	4.73	1.00	1.94	32.50	28.10
Vigor Dairy Feed	16.00	20.01	3.50	5.37	12.00	9.22
Vigor 16% Dairy	16.00	16.38	3.50	3.79	12.00	12.53
Washburn's Gold Medal Hard Wheat Standard						
Middlings and Wheat Screenings	15.00	16.42	4.00	5.16	9.50	7.99
Glidden Company **Indianapolis, Indiana**						
Glidden All Mash Layer	15.00	15.81	3.00	3.91	6.00	4.4
Glidden Laying Mash	20.00	21.63	3.00	4.35	8.00	5.96
D. H. Grandin Milling Co. **Jamestown, New York**						
Grandin's 14 Fitting Ration	14.00	15.45	3.5	4.81	9.00	7.28
Grandin's Horse Feed	9.50	10.81	3.5	4.27	11.00	7.13
Grandin's Laying Mash	20.00	21.58	3.0	4.94	8.00	7.88
Grandin's 16 Milk Maker	16.00	17.47	4.0	5.39	10.00	9.48
Grandin's Rabbit Pellets	17.00	14.45	3.0	3.72	10.00	14.56
Grandin's Start-To-Finish Mash	18.00	18.69	3.00	5.01	8.00	7.92
Grandin's Starter and Broiler Mash	18.00	18.21	3.0	4.51	8.00	6.94
Grandin's Stock Feed	9.00	10.15	4.0	4.68	12.00	10.45
Grandin's 18 Test Cow Ration	18.00	18.91	4.0	5.26	9.00	8.18
Green Acre Farms **Nazareth, Pennsylvania**						
Green Acres Alfalfa Meal	17.00	17.99	2.00	2.19	27.00	26.31
E. C. & W. L. Hopkins **Greenfield, New Hampshire**						
Granite State Breeder Mash	20.00	17.95	3.00	5.32	6.00	6.39
Granite State Chick Starter	20.00	16.93	3.00	4.01	6.00	6.29
Granite State Complete Mash	15.00	15.06	3.00	4.44	7.00	5.75
Granite State 20% Dairy Feed	20.00	20.79	4.00	5.17	10.00	8.24
Granite State Egg Mash	19.00	18.76	3.00	4.87	6.00	5.95
Granite State Growing Mash	19.00	17.78	3.00	5.27	6.00	5.98
Granite State Hog Ration	18.00	16.81	3.00	3.91	7.00	3.95
Page 16% Dairy	16.00	16.55	4.00	4.63	9.00	7.16
Page Dairy	18.00	19.35	4.00	4.68	9.00	7.29
Provender	11.00	10.33	4.00	3.65	10.00	6.21
International Milling Co. **Minneapolis, Minnesota**						
Blackhawk Wheat Bran	15.00	16.37	2.50	4.53	12.00	8.17
Blackhawk Wheat Standard Middlings	16.00	17.47	3.00	5.05	9.00	6.25

*Protein and fat not less than, crude fiber not more than.

14

Manufacturer	Pounds in 100 lbs. of Feedingstuff					
Brand	Protein		Fat		Crude Fiber	
	Guaranteed*	Found	Guaranteed*	Found	Guaranteed*	Found
Ralph P. Johnson & Son						
Potter Place, New Hampshire						
Johnson's Complete Laying Mash ..	15.00	14.80	3.00	4.25	8.00	5.36
Johnson's Dairy Feed	18.00	19.35	3.00	4.23	9.00	7.45
Johnson's Growing Mash	14.00	16.38	3.50	4.45	8.00	6.61
Johnson's Mash Feed	18.00	19.79	4.00	5.06	7.00	7.37
Johnson's Pig and Hog Feed	15.00	16.20	2.50	4.27	7.00	6.21
Kellogg Milling Co.						
Minneapolis, Minnesota						
Kellogg 16% Special Dairy Feed	16.00	16.24	5.00	5.78	8.00	7.88
Roller Ground Flaked Wheat	13.00	12.74	2.00	1.52	6.00	2.44
Keystone Dehydrating Co.						
Nazareth, Pennsylvania						
Keystone Super-Green Dehydrated						
Alfalfa Meal	17.00	17.29	2.00	2.03	30.00	30.31
Maine Fish Meal Co.						
Portland, Maine						
Maine Vitamin D Concentrate	50.00	50.52	15.00	18.59	1.0	0.39
Maritime Milling Co.						
Buffalo, New York						
B-B Broiler Ration	20.00	19.64	3.5	4.28	7.0	7.81
B-B Complete Chick Starter Ration ..	20.00	19.00	3.5	4.60	7.0	7.71
B-B Dairy Ration	18.00	19.30	3.5	4.76	9.0	7.54
B-B Egg Mash	20.00	20.35	3.50	3.99	9.0	7.67
Bull Brand B-B 20 Dairy Ration	20.00	24.73	3.5	4.29	9.00	9.57
Daisy Growing Mash	17.00	21.67	3.5	3.80	8.0	7.98
Dollar Maker Egg Mash	19.00	22.02	3.5	3.93	8.0	7.95
Hunt Club Dog Food	23.00	22.22	3.5	4.95	4.0	3.28
Merrimack Farmer's Exchange						
Concord, New Hampshire						
Merrimack All Mash	15.00	14.15	4.00	3.30	6.00	5.22
Merrimack Breeder Mash	19.50	16.58	5.00	3.73	6.00	5.27
Merrimack Calf Meal	20.00	21.36	4.50	4.22	5.00	6.04
Merrimack Calf Starter	18.00	16.68	4.00	4.30	4.00	6.26
Merrimack Chick and Broiler Mash ..	18.50	15.65	4.00	3.71	6.00	5.22
Merrimack Chick Starter	18.00	17.05	3.50	4.04	6.00	4.85
Merrimack Complete Layer	15.00	13.88	3.50	3.58	7.00	4.60
Merrimack 16% Dairy Ration	16.00	13.53	3.50	2.95	8.50	5.89
Merrimack Fitting Ration	14.00	13.90	4.50	3.75	8.50	6.44
Merrimack Goat Ration	14.00	12.05	4.50	3.29	8.00	10.01
Merrimack Growing Mash	17.00	16.29	4.25	3.64	6.00	5.32
Merrimack Hog Ration	15.00	13.86	4.00	3.31	7.00	6.87
Merrimack Horse Feed	11.00	11.99	3.50	4.25	6.00	7.51
Merrimack Laying Mash	19.00	18.26	4.00	4.38	6.00	4.77
Merrimack Pig Ration	17.00	15.30	5.00	3.54	7.00	6.24
Merrimack Turkey Growing Mash						
(Pelleted)	20.00	17.08	3.00	4.43	8.00	5.58
F. R. Miller Feed Mills						
Omaha, Nebraska						
18% Broiler Ration	18.00	18.12	5.00	4.05	5.50	7.47
18% Egg Mash	18.00	19.04	4.50	4.62	6.50	6.11
16% Growing Mash	16.00	18.79	4.50	4.51	6.50	6.08
George Q. Moon Co.						
Binghamton, New York						
Complete Laying Mash	16.00	15.36	3.00	3.69	9.00	6.79
Complete Laying Mash (Pelleted) ..	16.00	15.81	3.00	3.95	9.00	7.27

*Protein and fat not less than, crude fiber not more than.

15

Manufacturer	Pounds in 100 lbs. of Feedingstuff					
Brand	Protein		Fat		Crude Fiber	
	Guaranteed*	Found	Guaranteed*	Found	Guaranteed*	Found
George Q. Moon Co. Concluded						
Fitting Ration	13.00	15.54	3.00	3.62	9.00	6.29
Hog Feed	13.00	15.02	3.00	4.02	5.00	6.50
Special A Dairy 16% Ration	16.00	15.18	3.00	3.87	10.00	8.02
New England Grain Co. Portland, Maine						
New England Sweetened Horse Feed	9.00	13.53	3.00	4.34	9.00	9.18
New England 16% Test Ration	16.00	15.78	4.00	4.78	9.00	8.74
North Dakota Mill and Elevator Grand Forks, North Dakota						
All Mash Chick Starter and Grower	16.00	14.87	4.00	4.64	7.00	5.89
Dakota Maid All Mash Chick Starter and Grower	16.00	14.92	4.00	4.64	7.00	5.76
Dakota Maid All Mash Laying Ration	16.00	14.98	3.50	4.89	8.00	6.47
Dakota Maid Pig and Hog Feed	16.00	17.73	3.50	4.51	7.00	5.54
Dakota Maid Wheat Bran	13.00	15.24	3.50	5.69	12.00	10.55
Northwest Distributing Co. Colby, Wisconsin						
Northwest's 18% Broiler	18.00	18.08	4.00	3.87	8.00	6.37
Northwest's 23% Chick Starter	23.00	24.60	4.00	4.49	8.00	7.65
Northwest's 16% Dairy Ration	16.00	17.55	3.00	6.40	12.00	11.98
Northwest's 18% Dairy Ration	18.00	19.13	3.00	7.12	12.00	9.87
Northwest's 20% Dairy Ration	20.00	22.33	3.50	4.15	12.00	11.88
Northwest's 17% Laying Mash	17.00	17.86	3.50	4.62	8.00	8.54
Ogden Grain Co. Utica, New York						
Cloverbloom 20% Dairy Feed	20.00	17.58	3.50	4.99	12.00	9.77
Ogden Pig Feed	16.00	16.42	3.50	7.72	10.00	8.19
Pilgrim Layer and Breeder	20.00	18.85	4.00	5.78	7.00	6.87
Pilgrim Starter Grower Layer	18.00	18.65	4.00	7.10	8.00	7.99
Ogilvie Flour Mills Co. Fort William, Canada						
Ground Mixed Feed Oats	12.00	12.43	4.00	4.54	12.50	11.24
Oswego Soy Products Corp. Oswego, New York						
Old Process Expeller 41% Protein Soybean Oil Meal	41.00	43.91	4.00	4.92	7.00	5.54
Park & Pollard Co. Boston, Massachusetts						
All Mash Growing Feed	14.50	16.29	2.50	3.35	7.00	6.66
All Mash Laying Ration	15.00	15.50	3.00	4.13	7.00	6.29
Breeder Mash	18.00	19.44	3.00	4.49	7.00	5.73
Broiler Mash	16.00	18.30	3.00	3.99	7.00	5.07
Chick Starter	18.00	19.00	2.50	4.08	7.00	7.11
Doublex 16% Dairy Ration	16.00	18.83	3.50	4.46	12.00	10.49
Fitting Ration	12.00	13.97	3.00	4.87	9.00	7.24
Fleshing Pellets	16.00	17.29	2.50	3.33	7.00	6.99
Growing Feed	14.00	17.60	3.00	4.40	7.00	6.31
Lay or Bust Dry Mash	16.00	16.46	3.00	3.88	7.00	6.14
Milk Maid 16% Dairy Ration	16.00	19.70	3.50	4.20	10.00	8.52
Milk Maid 18% Dairy Ration	18.00	20.05	3.50	3.97	10.00	8.81
Milk Maid Fitting Ration	14.00	15.68	3.00	4.73	9.00	7.65
Milk Maid Test Cow Ration	16.00	17.20	4.00	3.93	9.00	8.73
Milkade Calf Starter Pellets	22.00	24.25	4.00	4.14	7.00	6.48
Rabbit Pellets	14.00	16.68	3.00	3.74	7.00	6.61
Stock Feed	9.00	8.17	2.50	3.23	12.00	11.93

*Protein and fat not less than, crude fiber not more than.

16

Manufacturer Brand	Pounds in 100 lbs. of Feedingstuff					
	Protein		Fat		Crude Fiber	
	Guaranteed*	Found	Guaranteed*	Found	Guaranteed*	Found
Park & Pollard Co. Concluded						
Turkey Grower	18.00	20.66	3.00	4.32	7.00	5.34
Turkey Starter	26.00	24.26	2.50	3.58	7.00	5.69
Yankee Horse Feed	10.00	11.86	3.00	4.51	9.00	7.97
Parrish-Heimbecker **Toronto, Canada**						
Parrheim Wheat Bran	15.00	16.11	3.50	5.57	11.50	11.36
Pillsbury Mills **Minneapolis, Minnesota**						
Pillsbury's Fancy Wheat Mixed Feed	15.00	17.21	4.00	5.09	8.50	6.79
Quaker Oats Co. **Chicago, Illinois**						
Ful-O-Pep Broiler Mash	19.00	20.53	3.50	4.90	8.00	7.73
Ful-O-Pep Calf Starter (Pellets) ..	20.00	20.31	4.50	5.49	8.00	5.86
Ful-O-Pep Chick Starter	17.00	18.78	4.00	5.62	8.00	6.25
Ful-O-Pep 16% Dairy Ration	16.00	17.91	3.50	4.26	10.00	9.74
Ful-O-Pep Egg Breeder Mash	20.00	20.84	4.00	5.44	8.00	6.62
Ful-O-Pep Fitting Ration	14.00	14.01	3.50	4.12	10.00	9.06
Ful-O-Pep Growing Mash	19.00	18.30	4.00	5.48	8.00	7.64
Ful-O-Pep Laying Mash	20.00	22.11	3.50	4.45	8.00	7.93
Ful-O-Pep Super Greens (Pellets) ..	19.00	19.04	4.50	5.46	8.00	6.22
Ful-O-Pep Turkey Grower (Pellets)	20.00	20.44	3.50	5.07	8.00	8.44
Quaker Sugared Schumacher Feed ..	10.00	10.98	3.00	3.06	12.00	8.90
Ralston Purina Co. **St. Louis, Missouri**						
Purina B & M Cow Chow	16.00	17.51	3.50	3.89	10.00	8.39
Purina Breeder Lay Chow	22.00	23.51	3.50	5.48	8.00	7.38
Purina Breeder Layena	15.50	15.67	3.00	4.09	8.00	5.26
Purina Broiler Chow	18.00	18.12	3.50	4.35	7.00	6.06
Purina Calf Startena	19.50	22.15	2.50	3.59	9.50	8.11
Purina Chick Chow	10.00	12.03	2.00	2.32	4.00	2.99
Purina Chick Growena	17.00	17.95	3.00	4.32	7.00	6.80
Purina Chick Startena	20.00	21.84	3.50	4.89	7.00	4.29
Purina Cow Chow	18.00	19.39	3.00	3.91	10.00	8.19
Purina Dry and Freshening Chow ...	12.50	12.96	2.00	3.97	14.00	8.68
Purina Goat Chow	16.00	16.85	3.50	3.79	10.00	6.37
Purina Hog Fatena	14.00	13.86	3.00	2.87	7.00	5.37
Purina 22% Lay Chow	22.00	22.59	3.50	4.18	8.00	7.53
Purina Layena	15.50	15.72	3.00	3.95	8.00	5.47
Purina Layena Pelleted ..../......	15.50	16.15	3.00	3.60	8.00	4.57
Purina Omolene	10.00	11.82	3.00	4.46	11.00	8.38
Purina Rabbit Chow Checkers (supplement)	16.00	17.82	3.50	4.64	8.00	7.47
Purina Turkey Fatena Meal	14.00	14.89	3.50	3.94	7.00	4.15
Russell-Miller Milling Co. **Minneapolis, Minnesota**						
Hard Wheat Occident Bran	14..00	17.16	4.00	5.13	11.50	9.59
Hard Wheat Occident Mixed Feed	15.00	17.86	4.00	5.47	9.50	8.22
Hard Wheat Occident Standard Middlings	15.00	17.60	4.00	6.19	9.50	7.94
Santa Ana Dehydrating Co. **Santa Ana, California**						
Alfalfa Meal	15.00	15.37	1.50	1.52	32.00	29.46
Saunders Mills **Toledo, Ohio**						
Vita-Greens Alfalfa Meal	17.00	16.84	1.50	1.75	30.00	26.69

*Protein and fat not less than, crude fiber not more than.

Manufacturer	Pounds in 100 lbs. of Feedingstuff					
Brand	Guaranteed*	Found	Guaranteed*	Found	Guaranteed*	Found
	Protein		Fat		Crude Fiber	
Schuyler Milling Co. Schuyler, Nebraska						
Grain Blend Feed	9.00	8.25	3.00	3.09	·6.00	2.0?
Puritan Egg Mash	17.00	12.12	3.50	3.22	7.00	6.4?
Sence Alfalfa Milling Co. Roscoe, California						
Sence Alfalfa Meal	17.00	15.27	2.00	2.01	25.00	25.74
Sherwin & Williams Co. Cleveland, Ohio						
Sherwin & Williams 32% Linseed Meal	32.00	34.81	4.50	8.68	9.00	8.1?
Sioux Soya Co. Soiux City, Iowa						
18% Egg Mash	18.00	18.39	4.00	3.78	7.00	6.8?
18% Growing Mash	18.00	17.64	4.00	3.62	7.00	6.2?
South End Hay and Grain Manchester, New Hampshire						
18% Dairy Feed	18.00	19.61	4.00	3.34	10.00	9.5?
Feedboard Egg Mash	19.00	21.10	4.00	5.81	7.00	8.0?
Feedboard Grower	17.50	20.14	4.00	5.47	6.50	8.5?
F. B. Spaulding Co. Lancaster, New Hampshire						
Spaulding's Dairy Feed	16.00	15.76	3.50	4.69	9.00	8.4?
Spencer Kellogg & Sons Edgewater, New Jersey						
Kellogg's Old Process Linseed Oil Meal	32.00	34.10	3.50	5.56	9.00	7.7?
A. E. Staley Manufacturing Co. Decatur, Illinois						
Staley's Corn Gluten Feed	23.00	26.35	1.50	3.69	8.00	5.7?
Stratton & Co. Concord, New Hampshire						
Fancy Wheat Bran	14.00	13.90	4.00	4.67	11.00	10.0?
Stock Feed	7.50	6.39	2.83	2.72	14.43	16.8?
Wheat Mixed Feed	13.50	14.58	4.11	4.74	7.13	8.0?
Sunshine Stores Fort Wayne, Indiana						
Local Mix Mash	15.00	19.35	3.00	4.88	·8.00	8.5?
Swanson-Plambeck Co. Rockford, Illinois						
Fieldcrest Super Broiler Mash	18.00	18.39	3.00	3.85	5.50	8.9?
Tri-State Milling Co. Rapid City, South Dakota						
Trisco Brand Wheat Bran	15.00	17.25	3.00	5.44	12.00	9.5?
Union Starch and Refining Co. Columbus, Indiana						
Union Corn Gluten Feed	25.00	27.49	2.00	3.29	8.50	7.1?
Unity Feeds Boston, Massachusetts						
Unity Breeder Mash	20.00	20.48	3.00	4.24	7.00	4.5?
Unity Chick Starter	18.00	18.61	3.50	4.69	7.00	4.8?
Unity Fitting Ration	14.00	16.50	3.75	4.28	8.00	5.3?
Unity Growing Mash	18.00	19.26	4.00	3.64	7.00	4.4?

*Protein and fat not less than, crude fiber not more than.

anufacturer	Pounds in 100 lbs. of Feedingstuff					
:and	Protein		Fat		Crude Fiber	
	Guaranteed*	Found	Guaranteed*	Found	Guaranteed*	Found
Unity Feeds Concluded						
nity Laying Mash	18.00	19.30	3.00	4.12	7.00	4.40
nity Pig and Hog Feed	17.00	18.33	4.00	4.18	7.00	4.37
nity Tri-Way Mash	15.00	17.25	4.00	4.14	7.00	4.98
nity Turkey Starting and Growing ash	22.00	20.38	4.00	4.23	7.00	4.58
Valley Dehydrating Co.						
Kingsburg, California						
e-Gee Fish-Trate	40.00	42.82	3.00	6.78	13.00	12.01
H. K. Webster Co.						
Lawrence, Massachusetts						
ue Seal All Mash Breeders' Ration	15.00	15.10	3.50	3.06	6.00	5.66
ue Seal All Mash Egg Ration	15.00	14.54	3.50	3.19	6.00	5.69
ue Seal Breeders' Mash	20.00	18.41	3.50	3.22	7.00	5.56
ue Seal Broiler Mash	20.00	19.76	4.00	4.60	6.50	6.17
ue Seal Calf Grower	12.00	12.69	3.00	3.81	12.00	8.04
ue Seal Chick Starter	19.00	19.15	3.50	3.74	6.50	6.06
ue Seal 16 Dairy Ration	16.00	15.24	4.00	3.26	9.00	6.90
ue Seal Egg Mash	18.00	17.08	3.50	3.61	6.50	5.27
ue Seal Fitting Ration	14.00	13.81	4.00	4.26	9.00	8.39
ue Seal Growing Mash	18.00	15.91	3.50	4.06	7.00.	5.52
ue Seal Horse Feed	10.00	11.42	3.00	3.84	9.00	7.11
ue Seal Pig Feed	15.00	15.19	3.00	3.52	6.00	5.31
ue Seal Scratch Feed	16.00	14.84	4.00	3.51	10.00	9.74
ue Seal Richford 16 Dairy Ration	10.00	10.81	2.50	3.35	4.00	4.40
ue Seal Stock Feed	8.50	10.94	3.00	3.20	17.00	8.72
Welco Feed Manufacturing Co.						
Spencer, Iowa						
elco Growing Mash	18.00	17.95	4.00	**3.32**	6.50	5.63
elco Laying Mash	18.00	17.70	4.00	**3.41**	6.50	5.76
Whitmoyer Laboratories						
Myerstown, Pennsylvania						
av-A-Dee	20.00	21.89	20.00	20.70	12.00	7.92

*Protein and fat not less than, crude fiber not more than.